RONA MUNRO

Rona Munro has written extensively for stage, radio, film and television including the recent adaptations of *My Name Is Lucy Barton* for the Bridge Theatre, London and Manhattan Theatre Company on Broadway, New York, and *Captain Corelli's Mandolin* for Neil Laidlaw Productions. She wrote the award-winning trilogy *The James Plays* for the National Theatre of Scotland, the National Theatre of Great Britain and the Edinburgh International Festival. This is the fifth play in that series about the medieval history of Scotland. The fourth, *James IV: Queen of the Fight*, premiered at the Festival Theatre, Edinburgh, in 2022, produced by Raw Material and Capital Theatres in association with the National Theatre of Scotland. *Mary*, a production for Hampstead Theatre in London, is the sixth.

Other credits include award-winning plays *Iron* for the Traverse Theatre and Royal Court London, *The Maiden Stone* for Hampstead Theatre, *Little Eagles* and *The Indian Boy* for the Royal Shakespeare Company, and *Bold Girls* for 7:84 Theatre Scotland.

Film and TV work includes *Oranges and Sunshine*, directed by Jim Loach and starring Emily Watson and Hugo Weaving, the Ken Loach film *Ladybird, Ladybird*, which won a Silver Bear at the Berlin Festival, *Aimée & Jaguar*, a Silver Bear winner and Golden Globe nomination, and BAFTA nominated *Bumping the Odds* for the BBC. She has also written many other single plays for TV and contributed to series such as *Doctor Who*.

Other Titles in this Series

Mike Bartlett
THE 47TH
ALBION
BULL
GAME
AN INTERVENTION
KING CHARLES III
MIKE BARTLETT PLAYS: TWO
MRS DELGADO
SCANDALTOWN
SNOWFLAKE
VASSA *after* Gorky
WILD

Jez Butterworth
THE FERRYMAN
THE HILLS OF CALIFORNIA
JERUSALEM
JEZ BUTTERWORTH PLAYS: ONE
JEZ BUTTERWORTH PLAYS: TWO
MOJO
THE NIGHT HERON
PARLOUR SONG
THE RIVER
THE WINTERLING

Caryl Churchill
BLUE HEART
CHURCHILL PLAYS: THREE
CHURCHILL PLAYS: FOUR
CHURCHILL PLAYS: FIVE
CHURCHILL: SHORTS
CLOUD NINE
DING DONG THE WICKED
A DREAM PLAY *after* Strindberg
DRUNK ENOUGH TO SAY I LOVE YOU?
ESCAPED ALONE
FAR AWAY
GLASS. KILL. BLUEBEARD'S FRIENDS. IMP.
HERE WE GO
HOTEL
ICECREAM
LIGHT SHINING IN BUCKINGHAMSHIRE
LOVE AND INFORMATION
MAD FOREST
A NUMBER
PIGS AND DOGS
SEVEN JEWISH CHILDREN
THE SKRIKER
THIS IS A CHAIR
THYESTES *after* Seneca
TRAPS
WHAT IF IF ONLY

Lucy Kirkwood
BEAUTY AND THE BEAST
 with Katie Mitchell
BLOODY WIMMIN
THE CHILDREN
CHIMERICA
HEDDA *after* Ibsen
THE HUMAN BODY
IT FELT EMPTY WHEN THE HEART WENT AT FIRST BUT IT IS ALRIGHT NOW
LUCY KIRKWOOD PLAYS: ONE
MOSQUITOES
NSFW
RAPTURE
TINDERBOX
THE WELKIN

Liz Lochhead
BLOOD AND ICE
DRACULA *after* Stoker
EDUCATING AGNES ('The School for Wives') *after* Molière
GOOD THINGS
LIZ LOCHHEAD: FIVE PLAYS
MARY QUEEN OF SCOTS GOT HER HEAD CHOPPED OFF
MEDEA *after* Euripides
MISERYGUTS ('The Miser') & TARTUFFE *after* Molière
PERFECT DAYS
THEBANS *after* Euripides & Sophocles
THON MAN MOLIÈRE

Linda McLean
ANY GIVEN DAY
GLORY ON EARTH
ONE GOOD BEATING
RIDDANCE
SEX & GOD
SHIMMER
STRANGERS, BABIES

Rona Munro
THE ASTRONAUT'S CHAIR
BOLD GIRLS
CAPTAIN CORELLI'S MANDOLIN *after* Louis de Bernières
THE HOUSE OF BERNARDA ALBA *after* Lorca
THE INDIAN BOY
IRON
THE JAMES PLAYS
JAMES IV: QUEEN OF THE FIGHT
THE LAST WITCH
LITTLE EAGLES
LONG TIME DEAD
THE MAIDEN STONE
MARY
MARY BARTON *after* Gaskell
MARY SHELLEY'S FRANKENSTEIN *after* Mary Shelley
PANDAS
SCUTTLERS
STRAWBERRIES IN JANUARY *from* de la Chenelière
YOUR TURN TO CLEAN THE STAIR & FUGUE

Stef Smith
ENOUGH
GIRL IN THE MACHINE
HUMAN ANIMALS
NORA : A DOLL'S HOUSE
REMOTE
SWALLOW

debbie tucker green
BORN BAD
DEBBIE TUCKER GREEN PLAYS: ONE
DIRTY BUTTERFLY
EAR FOR EYE
HANG
NUT
A PROFOUNDLY AFFECTIONATE, PASSIONATE DEVOTION TO SOMEONE (– *NOUN*)
RANDOM
STONING MARY
TRADE & GENERATIONS
TRUTH AND RECONCILIATION

Rona Munro

JAMES V: KATHERINE

NICK HERN BOOKS
London
www.nickhernbooks.co.uk

A Nick Hern Book

James V: Katherine first published in Great Britain as a paperback original in 2024 by Nick Hern Books Limited, The Glasshouse, 49a Goldhawk Road, London W12 8QP

James V: Katherine copyright © 2024 Rona Munro

Rona Munro has asserted her right to be identified as the author of this work

Cover artwork: design by Niall Walker; photograph by Mihaela Bodlovic

Designed and typeset by Nick Hern Books, London
Printed in Great Britain by Mimeo Ltd, Huntingdon, Cambridgeshire PE29 6XX

A CIP catalogue record for this book is available from the British Library

ISBN 978 1 83904 343 7

CAUTION All rights whatsoever in this play are strictly reserved. Requests to reproduce the text in whole or in part should be addressed to the publisher.

Amateur Performing Rights Applications for performance, including readings and excerpts, by amateurs in the English language throughout the world should be addressed to the Performing Rights Manager, Nick Hern Books, The Glasshouse, 49a Goldhawk Road, London W12 8QP, *tel* +44 (0)20 8749 4953, *email* rights@nickhernbooks.co.uk, except as follows:

Australia: ORiGiN Theatrical, *email* enquiries@originmusic.com.au, *web* www.origintheatrical.com.au

New Zealand: Play Bureau, 20 Rua Street, Mangapapa, Gisborne, 4010, *tel* +64 21 258 3998, *email* info@playbureau.com

United States of America and Canada: 42 M&P Ltd, see details below

Professional Performing Rights Applications for performance by professionals in any medium and in any language throughout the world (and amateur and stock performances in the United States of America and Canada) should be addressed to 42 M&P Ltd, Palladium House, 7th Floor, 1–4 Argyll Street, London W1F 7TA, *tel* +44 (0)20 7292 0554

No performance of any kind may be given unless a licence has been obtained. Applications should be made before rehearsals begin. Publication of this play does not necessarily indicate its availability for amateur performance.

www.nickhernbooks.co.uk/environmental-policy

James V: Katherine was co-produced by Raw Material and Capital Theatres and first performed at Capital Theatres' The Studio, Edinburgh, on 5 April 2024. The cast was as follows:

CONSTABLE/JAMES V	Sean Connor
KATHERINE	Catriona Faint
PATRICK/SPENCE	Benjamin Osugo
JENNY	Alyth Ross

FOR RAW MATERIAL

Writer/Executive Producer	Rona Munro
Director	Orla O'Loughlin
Executive Producer	Margaret-Anne O'Donnell
Executive Producer	Gill Garrity
Set/Costume Designer	Becky Minto
Sound Designer/Composer	Danny Krass
Lighting Designer	Derek Anderson
Associate Director	Eve Nicol
Movement Director/ Intimacy Co-ordinator	Janice Parker
Production Manager	Ali Low
Company Stage Manager	Naomi Stalker
Costume Supervisor	Nicky McKean
Associate Producer	Jana Robert
Marketing Manager	Niall Walker
Social Media Manager	Nicola Watson
Press Manager (Premier Scotland)	Joseph Crerar-Blythe
Historical Consultant	Dr Amy Blakeway
Historical Consultant	Ashley Douglas

FOR CAPITAL THEATRES

Chief Executive	Fiona Gibson
Senior Programmer	Munya Redman-Bayasi

For full Capital Team see www.capitaltheatres.com

RAW MATERIAL

Margaret-Anne O'Donnell and Gillian Garrity founded Raw Material, an award-winning, Scottish-based independent producing company in 2018.

'Our shared ambition to develop, create and tour bold accessible theatre that inspires, entertains and captivates audience across borders formed the foundations of our company. We are advocates for access and diversity within the sector and are passionate about enabling creative ambition, developing new models for success and supporting all stages of making theatre happen.'

Raw Material have produced and toured work of varying scale across Scotland, the UK and internationally, working collaboratively with a wide range of artists, companies and funders.

Productions include: *Love Beyond* by Ramesh Meyyappan, Raw Material and Vanishing Point; *James IV: Queen of the Fight* by Rona Munro, Raw Material and Capital Theatres in association with NTS; *The Stamping Ground*, lyrics by Runrig, book by Morna Young; *Arrangements* by John Kielty, Raw Material and Eden Court; *In the Interests of Health and Safety Can Patrons Kindly Supervise Their Children at all Times* by Raw Material and 21 Common; *Unicorn Christmas Party* by Sarah Rose Graber and Ruxy Cantir, Raw Material, Aberdeen Performing Arts, Eden Court Highlands, Capital Theatres; *Unicorn Dance Party* by Sarah Rose Graber and Ruxy Cantir, Raw Material; *The Signalman* by Peter Arnott, Raw Material and Perth Theatre; *Glasgow Girls*, book by David Greig, Raw Material in association with Regular Music; *We Are In Time* by Stewart Laing, Raw Material, Untitled Projects and Scottish Ensemble; *What Girls are Made Of* by Cora Bissett, Raw Material and Traverse Theatre Company in association with Regular Music; *After the Cuts* by Gary McNair, Raw Material in association with The Beacon Arts Centre; *Off Kilter* by Ramesh Meyyappan, Raw Material in association with Tron Theatre and Singapore International Foundation.

For upcoming productions and to support us visit
www.rawmaterialarts.com

Facebook: **raw_material_arts**
Instagram: **raw_material_arts**
X: **@RawMaterialArts**

‖‌‌ CAPITAL
‌‖‌‌ THEATRES

Capital Theatres presents world-class shows to entertain and inspire audiences of all ages. The three venues include two of Scotland's largest, oldest, and most respected theatres: Festival Theatre (1,915 seats), King's Theatre (1,122 seats, currently closed for a major redevelopment) and The Studio (155 seats). Together they host over 700 performances each year with a broad and inclusive programme featuring the very best in drama, dance, musical theatre, family shows, live music, comedy, and pantomime.

Capital Theatres is a receiving house which works with producers across the UK to programme their work. The organisation also commissions and co-produces a select number of productions of its own each year. Much of the programme is exclusive in Scotland, providing the only opportunity for audiences to see the biggest shows touring north of the border, the best in international contemporary dance and the latest productions from leading local and national companies. Capital Theatres is also the home of Edinburgh's largest community companies, providing them with a platform each year to share their work.

As Scotland's largest theatre charity, Capital Theatres supports access to the arts for everyone and has an extensive Creative Engagement programme of talks, workshops and events to introduce and develop participation and interest in the heritage of its buildings and all areas of live performance. Capital Theatres is also evolving an artist development programme, Open@TheStudio, and has won the UK Theatre 2023 Award for Excellence in Inclusivity for its work with people living with dementia.

www.capitaltheatres.com

Facebook: **captheatres**
Instagram: **captheatres**
X: **@captheatres**

*For Ashley and Amy
who so generously helped Katherine
stand on solid legs*

Characters

CHORUS 1
CHORUS 2
CHORUS 3
CHORUS 4
KATHERINE
PATRICK
JENNY
CONSTABLE
SPENCE
JAMES

This text went to press before the end of rehearsals and so may differ slightly from the play as performed.

A Chorus Addresses the Audience

CHORUS 1. In 1528 Scotland was a peaceful, united nation.

CHORUS 2. One people.

CHORUS 3. One Church…

CHORUS 4. One King…

CHORUS 1. Of course… the King was just a boy, his father was chopped to pieces on a battlefield. His mother turned from one man to another and lost herself altogether. He was raised by murderers.

CHORUS 2. But he's grown now. There's peace now.

CHORUS 3. The people of Scotland are poor and restless and struggling…

CHORUS 4. But they ay have been, ay will be…

CHORUS 1. The Church in Scotland is battered by critics.

CHORUS 2. Young men, daft boys…

CHORUS 3. Boys that have heard preachers in Europe… demanding reform…

CHORUS 4. But there's still only one Church. One God, one Church, one Pope…

CHORUS 1. As it's ay been…

CHORUS 2. As it ay will be…

CHORUS 3. Until one day… it isn't.

For a moment KATHERINE, *or* KATHERINE *and* JENNY, *are alone on stage. We see the shadow of memory on* KATHERINE, *memory of* JENNY, *it still preoccupies her as she moves into –*

Garden, Kincavel. Summer 1528

PATRICK *is in the garden. He looks round as* KATHERINE *comes into the garden.*

PATRICK. Good news.

KATHERINE. What?

As he says nothing.

What?

PATRICK. It doesnae matter.

KATHERINE. No, tell me.

PATRICK. We're *all* going to die. It's the only certainty.

KATHERINE. What… now?

PATRICK. No but…

KATHERINE. When?

PATRICK. One day. Inevitably.

KATHERINE. Before you're married or after?

PATRICK. Who knows?

KATHERINE. Because the wedding's tomorrow. If you know something you might want to let them know in the kitchen. There's a lot of soup going in that pot.

PATRICK. But think about it! Nothing else really matters, does it? We should… I should remember that.

KATHERINE. So… is this nerves or just a timely reminder?

PATRICK. What?

KATHERINE. I come out here, to pick flowers, for your lovely bride, you say 'Good news'…

PATRICK. Aye.

KATHERINE. And this is it? This is the good news? The inevitability of death?

PATRICK. Aye... because then you come to bliss.

KATHERINE. Right.

PATRICK. Probably.

KATHERINE. Probably?

PATRICK. Well who knows?

KATHERINE. God?

PATRICK. Aye! He does. For sure.

KATHERINE. As long as he does, eh?

Patrick, what are you doing out here?

PATRICK. Just... trying to be useful.

KATHERINE. They've sent you out the house, haven't they? Were you getting in the way?

PATRICK. Well... you know... there's a lot going on.

KATHERINE. It's a wedding.

PATRICK. Cooking and flowers and music and clothes and... cleaning.

KATHERINE. Aye. You're better out here. Cheering me up, with the idea of my grave.

PATRICK. It's just... in the face of death, what does it all mean? Food and flowers and music and clothes?

And we should always be ready *anyway*, shouldn't we?

KATHERINE. For death?

PATRICK. Obviously. It shouldn't be a worry. I mean... *no one* should ever be scared.

KATHERINE. Patrick, are you scared you're going to die?

PATRICK. But isn't everyone?

> And we shouldn't be. That's the thing.

KATHERINE. Are you planning on dying today?

PATRICK. No. Of course not.

KATHERINE. Because, you know, the bridegroom? There is a seat for you at the top table. I think we all thought you might say a few words.

PATRICK. That's the whole point of the day. Of course I'm making a speech.

KATHERINE. Preferably not about death.

PATRICK. No.

> (*Rallying*.) No. We're no there yet, eh? What am I thinking?

KATHERINE. I've nae idea.

PATRICK. And when I preach… who knows what'll come of that? If God inspires me…

KATHERINE. Inspires you to what?

PATRICK. To speak his truth! Even our enemies might be converted, eh?

KATHERINE. By your *wedding* speech?

> I was hoping you might say a few kind things about your bonny wee bride? Maybe a few…

PATRICK. What?

KATHERINE. Jokes?

PATRICK. I've never told jokes well.

KATHERINE. No. Just a thought.

PATRICK. I've to speak about my bride?

KATHERINE. Again, bridegroom? It's usually expected.

PATRICK. But I have to speak God's truth. There'll be people here tomorrow who've never heard it described. If I can make people understand that the Church must be changed...

KATHERINE *(cutting him off)*. They'd understand better if you could crack a joke, Patrick!

PATRICK. What are you saying?

KATHERINE. Look... I've read your articles.

PATRICK. And?

KATHERINE *(little hesitation)*. I...

I'm lucky, I've had an education...

PATRICK. *What are you saying?*

KATHERINE *(struggling)*. It's...

You're...

I don't think you can stand there... spouting *theology*... and expect most folk to understand what you're telling them.

PATRICK *says nothing*.

Sorry.

PATRICK. Crowds come to hear me preach, Katherine.

KATHERINE. Aye. *Students*.

Students love to shout about things no one else can understand.

I'm just saying you need to persuade the rest of us too.

As he says nothing.

Don't you?

PATRICK. You don't think I can do that?

KATHERINE. Not with your usual...

(Stops herself.) You just sometimes... overcomplicate things.

PATRICK. God is complicated.

KATHERINE. Well... then maybe a good preacher's job is to make him easier to understand. And anyway you're no giving a sermon! This is a wedding speech!

(*As he doesn't reply.*) Wait a minute... *wait* a minute! I thought this was a wedding? A real wedding?

PATRICK. It is.

KATHERINE. *Is* it though? Is it, Patrick? You told us this was a real marriage!

PATRICK. It is!

KATHERINE. Is this just an excuse to gather a crowd? A gathering of *your* faithful?

PATRICK. It's your faith too.

KATHERINE. But that's...

That's *dishonest*, Patrick!

PATRICK. Who am I lying to?

KATHERINE. Mother! Me! *Your bride!*

He thinks about it.

PATRICK. You're right.

Oh God you're right.

(*Alarming new thought.*) Katherine, I shouldnae marry at all.

KATHERINE. You have to marry! We've killed the pigs!

As he says nothing.

Patrick! You're marrying Jenny tomorrow!

JENNY *appears behind them. They both turn and look at her. She's in her wedding dress.*

Jenny.

Beat.

You look so different.

I mean... that's lovely.

JENNY. It doesnae fit, they're going to let it out.

KATHERINE. I know, but you still look...

JENNY (*cutting her off*). It's these bits...

(*Prods at them.*) My upper arms, they're too tight in the sleeves. I wish I didnae need sleeves, it's going to be so hot.

Looks at them.

It's good to see you, Patrick.

PATRICK. You too.

JENNY. It's good to see you, Katherine.

KATHERINE. Yes.

JENNY. I'm looking forward to tomorrow.

PATRICK. Aye.

A wee hesitation, then JENNY *leaves.* KATHERINE *is glaring at* PATRICK.

KATHERINE. *You cannae leave her on her wedding day!*

PATRICK. I'll talk to her father. We'll decide what's best.

KATHERINE. What's best is that you *make up your mind and keep it, Patrick*!

What's going on? I thought this was wedding nerves, if it's not that, why are you so...?

PATRICK (*cutting her off*). I'm finding the strength, to do my duty to God...

That's a duty far beyond what I owe family, or a wife.

KATHERINE (*annoyed*). Oh aye. Course it is.

PATRICK (*checks himself*). I'm sorry, I know for a woman that's everything. But I've got more to worry about. Things you can't... (*Stops himself.*)

Things you'll never have to face.

KATHERINE. As a woman?

PATRICK. We have different duties, don't we? God made it so.

KATHERINE. Aye. I know that.

PATRICK. And there's no happiness if we don't accept the duty God asks of us.

KATHERINE (*concedes*). Mebbe not.

> No. It just maks you… restless, eh? You cannae settle in your ain skin. Best no thinking of anything but duty. That's mair… peaceful.

PATRICK. What are you saying?

KATHERINE. I'm agreeing with you!

PATRICK. Are you not happy? In your marriage?

KATHERINE. I… Yes! Of course I am!

> I'm married to David Stewart, Captain of Dunbar Castle! That's…
>
> There are *hundreds* of souls in Dunbar. You don't pass the same face twice in the length of the High Street. It's a new world!
>
> I live alongside the Lady Seton… David's a royal servant! There'll be royal visits. We'll travel up to Edinburgh, I'll see the court, I'll see the court entertainment!
>
> Dunbar has a harbour full of ships that sail all the way to the *Mediterranean*.
>
> I'm lucky.

PATRICK. Is he… kind to you?

KATHERINE. He's fine.

> (*As* PATRICK *isn't reassured*.) He is, he's a good man. You know that.

PATRICK. Aye. He's strong on the need for Church reform. He's helped a lot, organising today.

KATHERINE. There you go. A perfect brother-in-law.

Maybe I just wish...

Mebbe I'd've liked God to need a greater duty from me.

PATRICK. Don't ask for that, you couldnae bear it. No woman could.

KATHERINE. Oh but you can?!

PATRICK. Aye! This is me, bearing it!

KATHERINE. Poor you. Poor wee bridegroom. Bearing *what*?!

PATRICK. This is what I understand now, Katherine. Any human soul only has two real choices. How we live and how we die.

KATHERINE. We're doing a choice of first course. Oysters or onion soup. Don't pick the oysters.

PATRICK. I just have to find the courage to make the right choice.

I think I'll be arrested, when I go back to St Andrews.

That startles her.

KATHERINE. No. *No!*

You've been invited back, the bishop himself...

PATRICK. I think it's a trap.

KATHERINE. Why would they *trap* you?

PATRICK*'s tone is suddenly urgent.*

PATRICK. Listen. *Listen.* I'm trying to tell you, I didn't realise... I should have realised... I didnae realise this moment would come so fast, that I might no be ready for it...

I think I will be arrested and I think I'll have to prove my faith. And... I don't know if I'm brave enough.

KATHERINE. For what?

He doesn't reply.

Patrick, what do you think is going to happen to you?

PATRICK. If God wills…

If God gives me strength, I'll find the words that change everyone's mind. That change the world. I can pray for that, eh?

KATHERINE. Patrick, they wouldn't dare arrest you. We're the Hamiltons of Kincavel! This family will keep you safe, always.

So you're stirring folk up with good argument! We're still cousins to the King, Patrick!

PATRICK. Aye.

KATHERINE. Well then, don't be worrying what some bishop in St Andrews thinks of you.

PATRICK. No. He's no authority over my soul, eh?

KATHERINE. There you go.

She shows him the bouquet.

What do you think?

PATRICK. Sweet and simple.

Like wee Jen.

KATHERINE. She's our neighbour, she's been your friend all her life. Be kind to her.

PATRICK. We had great games together, didn't we, the three of us, falling in the burn down there…

KATHERINE. Happy times, and we'll have more. You're worrying about nothing. You're safe here, you're safe in St Andrews. If anyone was going to arrest you they'd have done it long before this, you're an important man now, Patrick, but you're no that important. Get over yourself and put a flower in your hat!

PATRICK. Alright.

He leaves.

JENNY *comes on, still in her wedding dress.* KATHERINE *shows her the flowers.*

KATHERINE. Look. I'll mak a braw posy for you.

JENNY. Why didn't you send for me?

KATHERINE. When?

JENNY. When you moved to Dunbar?

KATHERINE (*taken aback*). I...

I didn't think you wanted that.

You could've visited. I'd've been glad to see you. Your father visited.

JENNY. You invited him.

You didnae invite me.

KATHERINE. You could've still come!

JENNY. I couldn't. Of course I couldn't.

KATHERINE. You'd've been welcome!

JENNY. Would I?

Why did you no write to me?

KATHERINE. You cannae read!

JENNY. Someone could've read it to me!

KATHERINE. You think? You think that would've been a good idea?

JENNY. I don't mean you should've written about wanting to kiss my neck! Just...

KATHERINE (*cuts her off*). Jenny, you're marrying my brother.

JENNY. I ken.

(*Bitter.*) That's lucky, eh?

KATHERINE. I am glad to see you.

I'm glad you're here.

A pause.

JENNY. Alright.

A pause.

KATHERINE. You should change out of that dress now, it's bad luck to be seen in it before the wedding.

JENNY. Right enough, I probably shouldnae risk even leaving my room the night before my wedding, eh?

JENNY *starts to leave.*

KATHERINE. What's that supposed to mean?

Jenny?

JENNY *doesn't answer. She moves into –*

A Bedroom at Kincavel, Evening of the Next Day

It's PATRICK and JENNY's wedding night. They look awkwardly at their wedding bed.

PATRICK. Alright.

Alright here we are so… can I ask you something? Will you be disappointed if we don't have our wedding night? I mean…

He indicates the bed.

JENNY. Oh.

PATRICK. Is that alright?

JENNY. Of course, aye, whatever you want.

PATRICK. You're disappointed.

JENNY. No. *No*, really, you're fine.

PATRICK. We won't have a lot of time, and it is my duty, to God, as a husband, so… if it's important to you…

JENNY. I honestly don't mind.

PATRICK. Well let's not.

JENNY. That suits me. I mean… long day.

So what'll we do?

PATRICK. Are you hungry? Because I was too nervous to eat but…

JENNY (*interrupts, relief*). I'm *starving*.

PATRICK. We can't… We can't send for food though, can we?

JENNY *has a hanging pocket or bag on her. She shows him.*

JENNY. I've got shortbread.

PATRICK. Oh I love you. Jenny, I truly love you.

JENNY *is breaking it in two.*

JENNY. I took it from the table. I knew I'd want it later. Here.

PATRICK. No you have the bigger half.

JENNY. No you! Go on, it's for you.

He takes it, he eats hungrily. JENNY *eats too.*

You spoke really well. You sounded very learned.

PATRICK *remembers*.

PATRICK. I was supposed to say nice things about you! Katherine told me to say nice things about you.

JENNY (*pleased*). Did she?

PATRICK. I forgot!

JENNY. Well… you could say them now.

He thinks she's serious, he's alarmed.

Joke.

PATRICK. I'm so sorry. About all this. I'm so sorry I've done this to you.

JENNY. Done what?

PATRICK. Married you.

JENNY. You're sorry you've married me?

PATRICK. In the circumstances.

JENNY. How do you mean?

PATRICK. Did your father not...?

> (*Struggles to explain.*) Your father and I planned this, this marriage allowed everything. It gave a reason for me to meet with him. Everyone was able to gather here without suspicion. I was able to speak without interference. Even the constables of the Church wouldnae stop a man talking at his own wedding.
>
> And this way you'll be provided for. My family will take care of you, if your father and brothers have to make a run for it.

JENNY. Run where?

PATRICK (*can't believe it*). Has no one talked to you about this?

JENNY. They don't really talk to me much. You know what my brothers are like.

PATRICK. Maybe they wanted to protect you...

JENNY. Why will they have to run from arrest?

PATRICK. Do you not even understand...?

> (*Sees she doesn't.*) We're all trying to reform the Church, Jenny, me, your father, your brothers, all the other men who gathered here. So all the bishops and the archbishops, all the officers of the Church call us heretics. They say we can be arrested for spreading terror.
>
> (*Hesitates, then breaks it to her.*) Jenny, I think it's very likely I'll be arrested.

JENNY. So why won't *you* run away?

PATRICK. Someone has to stand up first.

> What did you think of my speech?

JENNY. Aye! Like I said, very... learned.

PATRICK. But you understood what I was saying... about the Church... about what God requires us to understand?

JENNY. No really. Was I supposed to?

As he says nothing.

I'm sorry, I wasnae really listening, there's so many things you're not supposed to do when you're a bride. And this dress is so uncomfortable... I was just concentrating on not wriggling about.

PATRICK. I'm no preacher.

JENNY. No! You are! Everyone listened. I could see...

(*Finding the right words.*) My brothers thought it was very powerful.

PATRICK. Your brothers are persuaded already.

(*Realising.*) God wants more.

I knew that... But I don't know if I can do it...

JENNY. What?

PATRICK. Face execution.

JENNY. What...

PATRICK. I have to do it... my death would...

(*Struggles a moment.*) Public death is a powerful thing.

JENNY *takes that in.*

JENNY. It's a *horrible* thing.

You think you might be *executed*?!

No! Why are you saying this, Patrick?! Stop it! Stop it right now!

PATRICK. You have to understand me.

JENNY. I don't have to understand you! I do *not*!

PATRICK *has no answer.*

Explain it to me then. Explain yourself!

PATRICK. I'll be arrested. Then, if I can't persuade the court…

(*Working it out.*) No, my words won't persuade them. *Nothing* would persuade them. I already knew this. I knew this, Jenny, I *knew* this. I'm being weak. But it's clear, it's *clear* what I need to do.

They'll ask me what I believe, and I can't lie. I musn't lie. I won't lie.

JENNY. When they ask you what you believe about God?

PATRICK. Yes.

JENNY. And eternity?

PATRICK. Aye.

JENNY. And angels?

PATRICK. Mebbe not angels but… basically aye.

JENNY *takes that in*.

JENNY. I'd say I didn't know. I'd say I didnae know the truth about God and eternity and angels. It's *God*.

You're certain you know the truth about God and heaven?

PATRICK. Aye.

JENNY. How can you be?

PATRICK. It's a revelation.

JENNY. Like… a dream?

PATRICK. No I… I studied, I read, I listened to the great thinkers, Erasmus, Luther… this has been a long, long journey, but now, I'm sure. I'm certain. There's no escaping what I know.

And more than that… it's about what's right. Look at the corruption of the Church! The King is making his bairns, his bastards, into bishops to fill his treasury. Bishops are battling each other for gold. Priests who can't even spell their own names are still demanding every penny the poor ever earn. Do you understand?

The Church wants us enslaved in ignorance but if enough men study and learn for long enough... the shape of God's creation becomes clear. It's science, Jenny. It's logic. It cannae be denied. It has to be declared. Do you understand?

God has already decided our fate, we just need to believe in his will. That's the simple truth that'll free us all. Do you understand?

JENNY (*doubtful*). Mebbe.

PATRICK. All men stand equal before the Lord. There'll be no Pope.

JENNY (*disbelief*). No *Pope*?

PATRICK. Has your father not educated you?

JENNY. No.

He said as long as I can sew a straight seam.

I cannae though.

PATRICK. We need new truth.

JENNY. What was wrong with the old truth?

PATRICK. It wasnae true.

JENNY. You're certain.

PATRICK. I just said. Did you no hear me? Jenny...

JENNY. You might be killed? You *want* to get killed?

PATRICK. I don't want to!

JENNY. And what do you think that'll do to Katherine?!

Does she know about this?

PATRICK. She's studied the same books... She's strong in her faith too.

JENNY. She knows you're getting executed?!

PATRICK. I...

I suppose part of me still hoped it might not come to that.

She doesn't believe it'll come to that.

JENNY. Well it doesn't need to come to that!

PATRICK. You just heard what I said. Was it enough? Did you understand the terrible corruption of the Church?

JENNY. Some... but...

PATRICK (*cutting her off*). Then I need I need a clearer argument. I need to accept execution.

JENNY. *No!!*

PATRICK. If you saw me die...

JENNY. I'm no going to see you die!

PATRICK. *If* you saw me die, and I wasnae frightened, and I was just glad to be going to God, and I didnae shake, and I didn't cry and I just held to my prayers... would you still think I was mad?

JENNY. I'd think you wernae of this earth.

PATRICK. Part of God already?

JENNY. Something like that.

PATRICK. Aye. Here we go then, here we go.

Thank you.

JENNY. For what?

PATRICK. For showing me how it needs to be done.

Good.

Decided.

I was shaky there for a moment, I was, but... now I'm sure. That's a... *relief.*

Thank you, Jenny.

I'm happy now.

JENNY. No, Patrick, you're really scared. I can see you are!

PATRICK *doesn't answer for a moment, he's very close to breaking down.*

He tries to hold himself together.

PATRICK. Aye. Oh God forgive me.

JENNY *is near him. She's quietly trying to comfort him.*

JENNY. Oh Patrick…

PATRICK. Even the shortbread…

JENNY. The shortbread?

PATRICK. It's hard to lose the world, eh? I know what I need to do but… a bit of butter melting in my mouth and I lose sight of heaven. I'm pulled back to the ignorant pleasure of a mindless beast. Like the fat friars at the abbey beyond Kincavel, wiping stolen mutton fat from their chins and belching in the face of the Lord…

JENNY. I like the brothers.

PATRICK. They're sodomites, Jenny. Don't you know what that means?

JENNY. Of course. But… so are lots of folk. Aren't they?

PATRICK. It's a *sin*.

JENNY. Aye but… everything's a sin. We're all sinners. We confess and we're forgiven. Is there no forgiveness any more then?

PATRICK. No.

JENNY. *No?!*

PATRICK. Not for what goes against the natural laws of God. How could there be?

JENNY. Are there to be new laws too?

I cannae read but I know my commandments.

PATRICK. Good.

JENNY. So where does it say about sodomites?

PATRICK. They're unnatural. They're damned. It's clear.

JENNY. I'm sorry, I've always wondered if you....

PATRICK. What?

JENNY. Well... and you didnae want to take me to bed I...

PATRICK (*cuts in*). You thought I was a sodomite?

JENNY. Maybe?

Sorry.

PATRICK. No.

JENNY. It's just I heard that a lot of folk at the universities...

PATRICK (*cutting in*). Aye. But I'm not.

JENNY. Right.

Sorry.

PATRICK (*cutting in*). And it's all a distraction anyway, Jenny, shortbread, drink, dancing... all that other... carry-on. It doesnae get me to heaven.

JENNY. I thought that was heaven.

The melt of shortbread on your tongue...

The sun on your face the first morning there's light at the end of a winter night...

Holding someone's hand...

The feel of their fingers when you know there's love between you... That's *life*...

PATRICK. Aye, but how does any of that continue once we're in our graves?

JENNY (*that's an alarming idea*). Oh!

Oh right enough...

Oh Patrick... that's a scary thread to pull.

Will we no get shortbread in heaven?

PATRICK. It's...

We can't know.

I wouldnae have thought so.

I think, it'll be a... mair... significant kind o' bliss.

Beyond imagining.

Do you understand?

JENNY. If I don't will you stay alive to explain it better?

PATRICK. No.

JENNY. Doesnae matter then, does it?

You know... I thought there was a chance, a wee *teeny tiny* chance this would all come to happiness... somehow. How *fiel* am I?!

PATRICK. I'm sorry, you thought you were getting a husband.

JENNY. Well... I knew you'd be away a lot anyway so...

PATRICK (*laughs*). Aye, this is no so different. Katherine will take you into her household when you're alone.

JENNY. Aye. That's what I thought.

Have you ever watched those brothers? They come for our eggs, two gentle old men, I watch them walk away together. They carry the basket together. Sometimes Brother Paul carries the basket alone so Brother David can hold his hand. They support each other on the mud of the field. I love to watch them... such a long life and such tenderness between them...

(*Waits but he doesn't respond.*) Is it nuns too?

PATRICK. What?

JENNY. Will the men of your 'new truth' turn against the nuns too?

PATRICK. Only if they're corrupt.

JENNY. I really fancied being a nun. Katherine and me used to pretend we were...

A beat.

So you're to be arrested... my father and brothers will run away...

PATRICK. To England, aye.

JENNY. And... Katherine?

PATRICK. Oh they won't bother the women. Why would they?

I still can't believe... *All* of this should have been explained to you.

JENNY. Och that's alright. You've told me now. And I'm your wife, I'll still be a married woman, eh?

PATRICK *smiles*.

PATRICK. Are you happy about that?

JENNY. I'm a bairn no more, I can give my own orders in the kitchen. If I want pease soup I'll order pease soup and they'll have to make it, eh?

PATRICK. They will, you'll be mistress of the house.

JENNY. And mistress of you. I can speak my mind to my lawful chiel, in the time we have.

PATRICK. Of course.

JENNY. Good.

(*Suddenly serious and intent*.) Don't go getting yourself killed. There's no sense in a death like that when life is sweet. None.

I cannae bear to think about it, Patrick.

PATRICK. I know it's what God wants me to do.

A beat. She sighs.

JENNY. So how will we pass this night?

A beat. He has nothing.

We could play a game... not dice or cards but... how about fox and geese?

PATRICK *starts to laugh.*

PATRICK. Why not? God help me, why not?

But we've no board.

JENNY. We'll draw it on the floor with burnt wood.

She's getting this together. She's taking her wedding flowers apart.

We'll use... daisies for the geese... and this wee rose can be the fox.

PATRICK. I'll beat you.

JENNY. You won't, no one ever beats me. And don't think I'll let you win out of pity.

PATRICK *is suddenly very serious, urgent.*

PATRICK. Jenny, will you make me a promise?

JENNY. Aye, if I can.

PATRICK. Look after Katherine. Stay close by her. Help her bear it if they kill me.

JENNY. Of course.

PATRICK. Save her from any sorrow, if you can, save her.

JENNY. I will. Above any other duty, any other love, I *promise* you, I will save Katherine Hamilton.

PATRICK. Thank you.

I need to pray.

You draw out the board and I'll be with you in a minute.

PATRICK *goes to kneel and pray.*

JENNY *watches him for a moment, then she turns into –*

Garden, Kincavel a Few Weeks Later

KATHERINE *and* JENNY *are sitting in the garden listening to the* CONSTABLE, *a priest. He's come to potentially make arrests in the aftermath of Patrick's execution. He is very richly dressed. He comes to the point.*

CONSTABLE. So they burnt him. It took six hours but they got him killed in the end.

Neither KATHERINE *or* JENNY *say anything, can't say anything.*

Och I'm sorry... Long way from St Andrews and we've come quick. The news did get to you?

You knew he was deid, eh?

He's mainly talking to KATHERINE, *pretty well ignoring* JENNY.

KATHERINE. Yes.

CONSTABLE. You knew they burnt him?

KATHERINE. Yes.

CONSTABLE. Good, good.

Well, I'm sorry for you, an awfy thing, to lose your husband like that.

KATHERINE. Patrick was my brother.

CONSTABLE *looks at* JENNY.

CONSTABLE. *You're* the wife?

JENNY. Yes.

CONSTABLE. An awfy thing. I'm sorry to have to tell it.

Did you know he was fixing to get himself killed?

KATHERINE. No, I should have done. He tried to tell me. I didnae believe him. I didn't understand. I do now. I understand everything my brother was and what he meant, now.

A beat.

CONSTABLE. Well that's fine. Let's get this bit of the day's work done.

So, I need to speak to the man of the house?

KATHERINE. My brother's away. My other brother. John Hamilton.

CONSTABLE. That's the boy I need to talk to.

KATHERINE. He's away.

CONSTABLE. Run away, has he? Aye, he would, he would. We know the names of every man that heard your brother speak. We've caught some of them. They'll all be feart of a singeing now. But your husband will be with you yet, eh? Where's that brave man? David Stewart! Captain of Dunbar Castle! Is he about?

KATHERINE. Away.

CONSTABLE. Away. Aye. Thought he might be.

KATHERINE. He... He had business, in Oxford.

CONSTABLE. He's in *Oxford*?

KATHERINE. Yes.

CONSTABLE. All the way south in *Oxford*?

KATHERINE. Aye.

CONSTABLE. And are you expecting him hame?

Ever?

(*As* KATHERINE *doesn't reply.*) Well, he's mebbe happier doon there, eh? There's plenty in *England* who've turned from the true Church, eh? King Henry himsel... Loads of safe wee holes to hide in the kingdom o' Henry Eight.

JENNY. Berwick-upon-Tweed.

CONSTABLE. What about it?

JENNY. That'd be the best. I love it. Have you been? It's halfway between everything. I like that.

CONSTABLE (*to* KATHERINE). Is she feeling alright?

JENNY. I'm fine.

CONSTABLE. If you say so. So, who's here?

KATHERINE. My mother.

My sister-in-law here.

Our household.

CONSTABLE. Aye, we might need to talk to all of them right enough.

It didnae need to be this serious. You know? I mean your brother Patrick there… what was he thinking? I mean… what was he *thinking*?

I was there. I was there for the whole thing and I'll tell you now, it did not need to happen. I'm sorry to say it, but Patrick Hamilton, your brother, your husband, was a stubborn arrogant arse who could be living yet.

Hard for you to hear, I'm sure, but there it is.

I mean we told him he'd be arrested. We told him. He could see us at all his meetings, watching, listening. I took him aside myself, I said, 'We will come for you, son, we will, we have to, you know it. Now, you've made your point, you've been heard. Everyone's let off a bit of philosophical steam. Do yourself a favour and hud your wheesht now. Get yoursel to confession. Have a wee think about the love of the Mother Church and see if you dinnae realise you feel like her son yet.' There's nae need to be burning folk alive, there's nae *need*.

JENNY. So why did you burn him?

CONSTABLE. You think he gave us a choice?! How long were you married to the boy?

JENNY. We were married last month…

CONSTABLE. Well if you'd known him longer you'd have known a stubborn arrogant *arse*. He might as well have tied himsel to the post and lit the kindling himself.

Might have made a better job of it too.

Damp wood.

Sweet Mother of Heaven, what were they thinking?

Well, they were thinking when they showed him the post and the kindling, he'd realise they really meant it and recant sharpish.

Not your Patrick. Oh no. It's like he *wanted* martyrdom. Aye he probably did, eh? He was the type.

Rain never stopped, and the wood was wet already.

Six hours to burn him. *Six hours*. Can you imagine what it was like, watching that?

Och well I'm sure you have.

So! We're going to make this easy, ladies. You dinnae even have to say a word. Just kiss the rosary and we'll call it an affirmation of true faith.

Who's first?

JENNY *and* KATHERINE *look at each other.*

KATHERINE. My mother will do it. My mother never understood why Patrick had to…

She absolutely believes, as she always did.

She's inside. She's in her bed but they'll let you come to her.

CONSTABLE. Thank you. But let's get our business here finished first.

He offers the crucifix. They don't move.

Ladies, this needs doing. Quicker it's done the quicker you can get on with grieving. No one'll deny you your grief but let's get you safe from arrest first, eh? Come on.

Again, he offers the rosary.

KATHERINE. Jenny, do it.

JENNY. I don't know what I think.

KATHERINE. So do it.

JENNY. He wouldnae want that.

KATHERINE. He's no here, Jenny. And you shouldnae suffer for what you don't even understand.

That's a beat. Then JENNY *goes forward and kisses the rosary.*

CONSTABLE. Good girl. Good *girl*! You've brightened my day. You've put a smile on my face, you have, well done.

Holds out crucifix to KATHERINE.

Now you, Mistress Hamilton.

KATHERINE (*uncertain*). Can you go in to my mother next?

CONSTABLE. I'm in a hurry here, every second we delay, your soul's in jeopardy…

KATHERINE. Well save Mother's first! Bring her the comfort of the true Church. Or is that not what priests offer these days?

CONSTABLE. I don't like the sound of that, mistress. Are you questioning the authority of Rome too? Is that what you're doing?

KATHERINE *doesn't answer.*

(*Gentler.*) I know you've been hemmed in wi heretics, my darling. But you've a sweet face. I can see you still feel, in your heart, where godliness lies. I know you do. No woman needs to get herself mixed up in this carry-on. You're asking for more trouble than you could bear. Come on now.

KATHERINE. More than any woman could bear…?

She laughs.

God. He's ay listening, eh? I wished for a greater duty. And here we are.

JENNY. Katherine, what are you doing?

CONSTABLE. You don't understand what you're doing.

KATHERINE. No, what I understand, now, is Patrick.

CONSTABLE. Good for you. Some time when terror's not breathing doon our necks you can explain him to me.

KATHERINE. I can read. I can read well. I read all his thoughts. I've read them again, since. He left papers I…

CONSTABLE (*cutting her off, sharp*). Aye and we've confiscated the whole blasphemous heap. I'm at the end of my patience now. Come on.

He offers the rosary again.

KATHERINE. No. I don't think I can.

CONSTABLE. You have to.

KATHERINE. I failed him. I didnae believe he was in real danger. I didnae see how brave he was. I…

I won't fail him again. I believe everything my brother said and wrote and preached, all of it. If he's a heretic so am I.

CONSTABLE. *Oh why did you have to say that?!?*

JENNY. Katherine…

KATHERINE. I failed him in life, I'll no fail him after!

CONSTABLE. Well I've heard you now, eh? I've heard you say it! Half of Kincavel probably just heard you say it?! What do you think I'm going to do now?!

KATHERINE. I don't care what you…

CONSTABLE (*cuts her off*). I'm going to have to arrest you, eh?!

JENNY. No! No you don't have to bother with the women. Patrick said…

CONSTABLE (*cuts her off*). Well I do if there's no one else here and the women are shouting *heresy*! What did you think I'd do?!

KATHERINE *is thrown.*

Right, I can see you didnae think it through. Let me spell it out. You need to take that back, what you just said, else I'll need to arrest you, and all the rest. The rest being the death your brother suffered. So… (*The crucifix.*)

Come on.

KATHERINE. He was brave. My brother was *so* brave. And I cannae deny the truth he taught me just to save my toes a singeing.

CONSTABLE. It'll be more than your toes, mistress.

And you'll feel every lick of flame, as he did.

You'll have seen it. In your mind's eye.

The greatest mercy you'll get, mebbe, mebbe if you've not made yourself irritating to all that tried to help you, is they might let you put gunpowder in your pockets.

One blast might take most of you before your pretty face is screaming charcoal. Otherwise it'll be a long, hard road to hell.

Right enough though, eh? If you're to be screaming and burning for all eternity what's an extra hour? Gie you a chance to get used to it.

KATHERINE. Well.

You know how to paint a picture, eh? You're a powerful preacher altogether. I bet you draw the crowds.

CONSTABLE. Eh?

KATHERINE. I bet the church was full when you were talking, Father. What was your biggest crowd? What would you guess? A hundred bums on pews? Three hundred?

The CONSTABLE *says nothing.*

How many saw Patrick die? Eight hundred was it?
A thousand?

Still nothing.

And he preached till the end, didn't he?

CONSTABLE. Until his throat burnt out. Aye.

KATHERINE. Six hours. Dying and preaching and never recanting his faith. That's a powerful argument. He persuaded me, as you see.

A stand-off.

CONSTABLE (*sighs*). *Peas in a bloody pod!*

Oh I did not need mair of this. I did not.

Fine then. I'll arrest you.

You'll be taken to Edinburgh. To court. To the ecclesiastical court. You'll be accused. Your truth will be tested.

KATHERINE. You'll torture me.

CONSTABLE. Your truth will be interrogated, in front of the men of the Church, the men of the parliament, the King… and then you'll be executed.

KATHERINE. I might be innocent though, eh?

CONSTABLE. Will you affirm the true faith?

KATHERINE. No. Only my own.

CONSTABLE. Then you're no innocent and you'll burn.

KATHERINE. Alright then. Good, we've got a plan. Will I pack?

CONSTABLE. You can say goodbye to your mother.

JENNY. I'll come with you.

(*To the* CONSTABLE.) She'll need a woman with her, to help her, her hair, her clothes, all the things…

CONSTABLE (*cutting her off, impatient*). Aye, aye, come along if you must.

JENNY (*as* KATHERINE *stares at her*). Let me come with you.

KATHERINE. Jenny, you're no my servant.

JENNY. Let me help you. Let me be with you. I want to.

KATHERINE. Alright.

And we're straight into –

A Locked Room in Holyrood Palace, Two Days Later

They've only just been put in the room. JENNY *is looking around.* KATHERINE *is lost in her own tense thoughts.*

JENNY. It's no so bad, is it? I mean, it doesnae feel like a prison.

KATHERINE. No.

JENNY. Just like a room. It's quite a nice room actually. Do you think?

    KATHERINE *doesn't respond.* JENNY *looks out the window.*

    Great view.

    I've never been to Edinburgh before.

KATHERINE. I know.

JENNY. Is the King mebbe just through that wall?

KATHERINE. Mebbe.

JENNY. Cannae believe it.

    JENNY *is looking up to the High Street.*

    Look at them all. You can see everyone from up here, eh?

KATHERINE. You can see more from the castle. Half of Scotland.

    I thought we'd be in the castle dungeon. So I suppose this is good – that they've put us in the palace instead. No instruments of torture in the palace.

    Mind you... a lot of them are pretty portable, eh?

JENNY. That's why I'm here. I won't let any of those bastards hurt you. Not one fingernail. Not one eyebrow hair. Let them try.

    KATHERINE *snaps.*

KATHERINE. Oh you'll stop them, will you? How will you manage that?!

JENNY *is working at something by the window.*

What are you doing?

JENNY (*still working*). The door's locked.

KATHERINE. Of course the door's locked.

JENNY. But we could maybe get out this window.

KATHERINE. We're two floors up!

JENNY. I've jumped from higher... well, almost as high.

KATHERINE. There's guards all round the front of the palace!

JENNY. I can run fast. You used to run fast.

KATHERINE. And where could we go?!

JENNY. Berwick-on-Tweed.

As KATHERINE *has no answer.*

It's great there. (*The window.*)

KATHERINE. It's the only place out of Kincavel you have ever seen.

JENNY. Until now.

Alright.

I just think we should try.

I think we should try something.

I mean they're no going to kill you but...

KATHERINE (*cutting her off*). They are going to kill me.

JENNY. No, they won't...

KATHERINE. They will! Did you not hear the Constable? They're going to kill me if I don't recant!

JENNY. So recant! It's just words!

KATHERINE. Patrick died for those words!

JENNY. Aye! So that job's done! No need for you to do it too!

KATHERINE. I'm his sister. If I cannae keep the faith…

This is my duty, now.

There's no one else left.

JENNY. Aye, because they *ran away*. All the men ran away rather than face this, but *you're* going to take it on?

KATHERINE. Patrick didnae believe I could do this.

No one thinks I can do this.

Well… they'll see.

He would've been proud of me.

JENNY. Proud you're as gyte as he was?

KATHERINE. Stop it…

JENNY. I loved him too but he wasnae right, Katherine! He never was. He couldnae even eat a bowl o soup! Sitting there with a book propped up, spilling it oer his front. He would fall intae a room like he didnae know how a door worked and fall oer a chair trying to sit on it…

KATHERINE. *You don't get to say that, Jenny!*

JENNY. Aye I do! I was his wife!

And I was his friend before that.

And I miss him.

This is suddenly too much for KATHERINE.

KATHERINE. I cannae, don't.

I didnae believe him. I didn't believe they'd really arrest him… kill him.

JENNY. No, nor did I. No really.

KATHERINE. So I cannae let him down now.

JENNY. He'd want you to live.

KATHERINE. He'd want his words to live.

A pause.

JENNY. You mind when we were playing hide-and-seek? And we hid up the tree?

KATHERINE *does, a happy memory.*

KATHERINE. I don't think he was ever looking for us.

JENNY. No, just wanted the noisy wee girls out of his hair. Then sat under that tree with his book.

KATHERINE. I don't think he'd've noticed us yet if I hadnae dropped a whole branch on him.

JENNY. Because he didnae notice the twigs, he didnae even notice the *beetle*, that might be in his hair yet.

KATHERINE. And the look on his face when he peered up at us...

JENNY. 'Who are you? Do I even know you?'

KATHERINE. Wandering away to find a quieter seat... Oh God...

He was never living in the same world as the rest of us, was he?

JENNY. No, so you need to recant now, Katherine, no one will judge you if...

KATHERINE (*cutting her off*). You need to distract me.

JENNY. Eh?

KATHERINE. What do you think you're here for, Jenny? To comb my hair?! I cannae be thinking about all this! I'll go mad!

JENNY. Well... come and look out the window then?

KATHERINE. I don't want to look out the window!

JENNY. We could... play a game or...

KATHERINE. A *game*?!

JENNY. Well I don't know! We could try!

Come on.

She stands, one hand behind her back, the other curved into a 'goose' neck.

KATHERINE. What are you...?

(*Remembers.*) The swan game.

JENNY. Geese. We decided it was geese.

KATHERINE *is taking up the same position.*

Because swans are bonny, but they're cruel.

Swans are horrible.

Geese are loyal and true. They fight for love.

JENNY *lunges at* KATHERINE, *trying to hook her arm round hers. This is the game, one arm has to stay up, the other behind the back, they take turns attacking and defending, the attacker is trying to 'hook' the defender's arm, the defender is dodging.* JENNY *is attacking first.*

You've forgotten how to do this, eh?

All through this JENNY *is attacking.*

You forgot a lot of things, Katherine. Seems like you maybe forgot me altogether.

KATHERINE. That's no fair.

I've had a lot to think about.

JENNY. Like what?

KATHERINE. Like learning what it means to be a wife!

JENNY. Oh aye, lolling aboot in Dunbar, eating scones with the Lady Seton.

KATHERINE. I've had to run a household! I've had to... learn what my husband wanted...

JENNY. What about what we wanted?

KATHERINE. That's just... what children do. Wee quines, playing at love. I'd my duty to think about.

He wants an heir, Jenny!

JENNY. Does he?

Well... he's run off to England, eh? Good luck making babies now.

JENNY *successfully 'traps'* KATHERINE. *She lets her go again.*

Your turn.

KATHERINE. Anyway... I didnae think you wanted me to send for you.

JENNY. How could you think that?

KATHERINE. Because you never came! I waited for hours under that tree! I caught a chill! I was sneezing through my wedding, David Stewart nearly pushed me back at my father because he was feart I'd die on him before the church!

JENNY. That wasnae my fault!

KATHERINE. You promised me! You promised you'd be with me that night! Just that last night when I was so scared about my wedding...

JENNY. My father guessed what we were doing.

KATHERINE. What?

How?

JENNY. Mebbe we wernae as secret as we thought. We didnae always worry if anyone was looking did we?

He locked me in. The wee linen press, upstairs. I got out the window in the end. I jumped. Not as big a jump as the windy here, right enough...

And I hurt my ankle.

I was slow.

If you'd waited a bit longer, I'd've come to you. You should've known I would.

KATHERINE. I thought...

You were so angry with me! When I told you I was marrying...

JENNY. I wasnae angry I was...

They've stopped 'playing' at some point in this exchange, but now KATHERINE *'catches'* JENNY, *cutting off her line.*

KATHERINE. Well now you know what happens when your father tells you you have to marry. Now you understand that you cannae just say no.

JENNY. I was glad to marry Patrick.

KATHERINE. Were you?

JENNY. It brought me back to you.

They're still linked together.

KATHERINE. It's against nature, what we did.

JENNY (*scoffs*). No it's no. Half the lassies of Scotland are unnatural if that's true.

KATHERINE. But they grow out of that! We're no bairns, Jenny. It's against our natural duty as women.

JENNY. So they tell me.

They nearly kiss. KATHERINE *breaks it.*

KATHERINE. We cannae...

JENNY. Katherine...

KATHERINE. We musn't. I need to be getting ready.

JENNY. Just let me...

KATHERINE (*cutting her off*). Mebbe I could tell jokes.

JENNY. Jokes?

KATHERINE. To stop them killing me. Am I funny?

JENNY. No really.

KATHERINE. Aye I *am*. I cannae talk like Patrick... but I can talk. I can... entertain...

JENNY. Patrick didnae even really *get* jokes, I don't think.

KATHERINE. No.

His words… they're like a battering ram at the castle gate. When enough folk repeat them that gate is coming down. That's true. He'll break all their walls in the end.

But if he could have hidden those ideas in a joke…

A joke is like sending in a secret spy that sneaks over the wall and opens the gate for you. And after… nobody's deid.

If a young woman made you smile you wouldnae want to see her set on fire, would you?

JENNY. No, *I* wouldnae. But some folk are that cruel…

KATHERINE. *Not helpful!*

JENNY. I think you should recant.

KATHERINE. No.

I can't.

Patrick said everyone really only has two choices, how they live and how they die…

But I'm no brave enough to die.

I can try.

I can try to…

I could mebbe… charm them all?

JENNY. You could charm a crab oot its shell, a squirrel oot its dray… all the wee birds oot the sky to walk at your feet.

JENNY *is close to* KATHERINE, *touching her.*

You just remember bairns' games?

I remember catching you at the back of the stable, the straw prickling our bare legs as I pushed my way up your skirt, up that softest stretch o' your hurdies, slowly, douce and feart, lest you push my hand down and awa, but you didnae, you grabbed it and pulled it right up to the heat o' you.

Remember?

I remember lying curled in your bed, the other women round us, servants and family all breathing and snoring and sleeping as we moved so slow, so quiet that they never knew what we did, even when it was done.

Remember?

KATHERINE (*quiet*). Yes.

JENNY. I remember lying at the back of the orchard, pinned by your mou, and I couldnae bear the heat of it, I couldnae bear the tug and push of your mou, your tongue darting into me, so good, so braw I was begging and begging you to stop because the pleasure would kill me deid, it was gonnae destroy me. And you didnae stop. And I was destroyed. I died and was born, new, under you.

KATHERINE (*struggling*). God made us to love him and do our duty to...

JENNY (*cutting her off again*). You made me! You made me into this Jenny here! The Jenny that's no fit to live withoot you!

A moment, then KATHERINE *kisses her.*

Don't you dare go getting yourself burnt! Don't you *dare*!

They kiss again.

The door opens and they spring apart. SPENCE *is there, he is a very young ecclesiastical lawyer. Again, he is very richly dressed. He is the servant of the bishop who has ordered* KATHERINE'*s arrest. He is in a controlled but agitated state.*

SPENCE. Hullo.

They say nothing.

If you don't mind, before we go down, I have some questions, about your brother... How long had the Devil lived in him. I mean I was there, I saw him burn. It's very troubling. I'm sorry... that's not a nice thing to ask. I mean I could not do that. I canne think of another explanation, he must have been possessed.

I mean...

I was there, I saw...

It's very troubling.

Did you see it? Did you notice when the Devil entered your brother?

I'm sorry... That's no a nice thing to ask but... that must have happened, I mean.

So I cannae think of another explanation. He must have been possessed.

KATHERINE. Who are you?

SPENCE. Oh! I'm the appointed officer of the ecclesiastical court. I'm the prosecutor.

KATHERINE. Whose prosecutor?

SPENCE. Your prosecutor. For the trial.

So you didnae see the moment the Devil came into him?

KATHERINE. No.

SPENCE. Right then, sorry to ask.

(*Remembers.*) Oh! Yes, another thing I was to ask, who sent word to the university?

KATHERINE. About what?

SPENCE. Your trial. There's a lot of students gathering in the High Street, Edinburgh boys, and from St Andrews... if that's your doing... well it won't help your situation. I was told to tell you that.

KATHERINE. I don't know anything about any students. Plenty folk know you arrested me. You didnae keep it secret, did you?

SPENCE. Probably should have done.

Hindsight, eh? No helping it now.

He waits expectantly.

So, you need to come?

KATHERINE. Now?!

SPENCE. Aye.

JENNY. The trial's *now*?

SPENCE. Aye...

Sorry, shall I give you a minute? If you need to...

Thing is, it can be a long day, best go now if...

KATHERINE. I don't need a minute. Thank you.

SPENCE. Good, good! Off we go then.

He ushers them into –

The Courtroom

KATHERINE *is taken to her place in the court.* JENNY *moves to a place nearby, ready to help her as appropriate, a dutiful lady's maid.*

SPENCE. In the name of God I call you all to witness. This ecclesiastical court is now in session.

He waits until the court has settled. He turns to KATHERINE. *He is anxious, tense, the scale of the occasion is huge, but he's keeping it under control.*

Katherine Hamilton, you stand before this court accused of the crime of heresy.

KATHERINE. So it seems.

SPENCE. A crime that would condemn both your life and your immortal soul. I am to question you on the truth of this accusation.

KATHERINE. And I swear by God in Heaven and by my immortal soul that I will speak nothing but the truth in this court.

So ask away.

SPENCE. You are accused of adherence to the same heretical articles proposed by your brother, Patrick Hamilton, promotion of which led to his conviction and execution for heresy.

He pauses as if waiting for her to say something.

KATHERINE. Sorry, was there a question there?

SPENCE. No... I...

KATHERINE (*cutting over him*). Because I know all that. And here I am. Just me. A woman all alone. Ready for your questions.

SPENCE. There's no need to be afraid.

KATHERINE. Glad to hear it.

SPENCE. Just answer, honestly, as God would want you to.

KATHERINE. That's the plan.

SPENCE *holds up papers.*

SPENCE. You know what these are?

KATHERINE. Papers, writing.

He brings them to her.

My brother Patrick's writing.

SPENCE. His articles of faith, heretical articles, writing that contradicts the teaching of the Church.

KATHERINE. If you say so.

SPENCE. Have you read these articles?

KATHERINE. Aye.

SPENCE. Good, I'm going to ask you if you agree with what your brother wrote. All you have to do is deny that you do. Do you understand me?

KATHERINE. You're very clear.

SPENCE. Good.

Alright.

Do you agree with what your brother asserts in these blasphemous articles?

KATHERINE. Which bit?

SPENCE. I'm sorry?

KATHERINE. Which bit of his writing are you asking about?

SPENCE. All of it! Any of it!

KATHERINE. There's a lot of spelling mistakes.

And there's bits when you cannae quite mak it oot. His handwriting was ay a trial to all of us. Did you find that?

As SPENCE *says nothing.*

You could make it all out, every word?

SPENCE. Yes.

KATHERINE. You've better eyes than me then.

SPENCE. I'm going to put this to you another way.

KATHERINE. I wish you would.

SPENCE. Will you recant?

KATHERINE. What does that mean?

SPENCE. What does 'recant' mean?

KATHERINE. No, I know what the word 'recant' means. It means you want me to deny a philosophy, a faith I may have once believed.

SPENCE. Exactly.

KATHERINE. What do you want me to deny?

SPENCE. *These papers! This writing!*

KATHERINE. I just told you, I cannae speak to every word because…

SPENCE (*interrupts*). Your brother asserts that the merciful work of God's servants is of no use at all. He says that babes are not saved by the priest's baptism, he says that a man's confession to a priest cannot save him from God's judgement, he says that God has already ordained all the good and evil in the world and a priest is not saving their souls, only deceiving them. He says the Pope is the Antichrist!

KATHERINE. I can see that's really annoyed you.

SPENCE. And do you agree?

KATHERINE. I'm no annoyed, no, I can stand to hear that.

SPENCE. Katherine Hamilton, you stand before God, in the presence of your king…

KATHERINE (*little curtsy*). Aye, His Majesty… my second cousin.

SPENCE. Do you understand why we're gathered here?

KATHERINE. It's a rainy day in Edinburgh, who'd be outdoors?

SPENCE. You're mocking God!

KATHERINE. I would never mock God.

You're fair game though, eh?

SPENCE. I'm God's servant. I cannae be mocked.

KATHERINE. If you say so.

SPENCE. Why are you…? Do you not understand you could be damned for what you're doing?

KATHERINE. I thought I was damned already.

SPENCE. Will you stop me doing my work?

KATHERINE. How can I stop you?! For the love of God, do your work! I'm sure I wish you were done with it.

SPENCE. Here then! Here!

He shows the papers to her.

Tell me if you see truth in one blasphemous word on this page!

KATHERINE *takes them, pretends to skim them.*

KATHERINE. I've read these many times. But I'll look again, here, before God, in the presence of my king, in the company of the great and good of Edinburgh. I'll read. I think I'm in *good* company here, friends, *family* even, men and women that understand that ideas are fish that fatten and swim, and change like elvers to eels, as agile as the minds God gave us to know truth. I mean, this is Edinburgh, this is the King's place, folk here know how to try on new ideas with the same grace they'd try on a new hat. I can see it in their faces... and their hats.

SPENCE. So this heresy is known. Written down by the blasphemers.

KATHERINE (*points*). Look, is that not an amazing hat?

SPENCE (*ignoring that*). It's here for anyone to read and will be entered in the court record. You've already read every word. You admit that.

KATHERINE. Aye. But.

SPENCE *takes the papers off her.*

SPENCE. So which of these articles do you affirm?

KATHERINE. Can I take another wee look at number eight?

I don't know, but it's worth a conversation, do you not think?

SPENCE. We're not having a debate here.

KATHERINE. Well there is though.

SPENCE. Listen to me, *listen* to me... If you affirm those articles then you're guilty in the eyes of God and man.

KATHERINE. No argument about it?

SPENCE. None.

KATHERINE. Well then there'll be a sign any minute then, eh?

SPENCE. What sign?

KATHERINE. If I'm such a heretic, God will probably strike me doon wi a lightning bolt, eh? That's traditional.

SPENCE. What?

KATHERINE. Though I'll be prepared to see his rage in any sign. Deid pigeon dropping from the rafters. I'll go with that.

Dog running howling from my damned satanic reek. See now I've said that I'll take a dog howling.

(*Listens.*) Can you hear one? No.

(*Looking round.*) How about... *how about*... there's a wee moth up there, look! See it! I can see it, bobbing about looking for a bit of good wool cloth to snack on. If that moth, *if that moth*, flies out the door rather than thole my ungodly breath, I'll believe my God has damned me already and Jesus himsel cannae save me... Look, look look! There it goes...

She follows its progress.

Think it's stopped in the curtain there. What does that mean, Father? Can you tell us?

SPENCE. You're mocking the power of Christ your saviour!

KATHERINE. No. That'd be blasphemy.

SPENCE. We all heard you!

KATHERINE. Aye. Mocking you. Are you Christ my saviour then?

SPENCE. Alright. You can mock me. Go ahead.

I'm trying to *help* you!

You've read these articles. You understand them. This is the moment, Katherine. I cannae make it plainer. I cannae do more to save your soul. We're waiting on your answer, a straight answer. Think about what you say next, *please*.

Do you reject this blasphemy or are you condemning yourself as a heretic like your brother?

Will you really burn?!

KATHERINE. Oh here we go then, here we go again, I... Oh, here we go then, here we go.

Suddenly she can't speak. JENNY *is on her feet, her eyes fixed on* KATHERINE.

SPENCE (*quieter*). Recant. Or we will kill you. We'll have to.

KATHERINE. I...

JAMES *suddenly stands up, applauding.*

JAMES. What a cliffhanger! Perfect! This is great, that is just bloody brilliant, ladies and gentlemen, don't you agree? Right we're going to take a wee break while I hear a bit more from the accused. You cannae blame me, eh? She's great entertainment.

SPENCE *is really rattled.*

SPENCE. Your Majesty, the court is in session.

JAMES. Whose court?

SPENCE (*thrown*). The... this is the ecclesiastical court... the judgement of God's appointed...

JAMES (*cutting in*). Aye, silly me, let me put that another way. After you've served God what is your duty to your king?

SPENCE *is speechless,* JAMES *answers for him.*

Obedience. We'll take a wee break.

He jerks his head at KATHERINE.

Come on, you, away through here and we'll have a word.

SPENCE *can only watch as* JAMES *leads* KATHERINE *into –*

King's Rooms, a Few Moments Later

JENNY *has followed.*

JAMES *is getting a glass of wine for him and* KATHERINE.

JAMES. So the world *is* ending. That's clear. Don't you think?

KATHERINE *doesn't know how to respond.*

KATHERINE. I...?

JAMES. I've high hopes of seeing the end of days. Don't you?

Well no you won't, because you'll be deid by tomorrow night. Or maybe...

(*Thinks.*) What day is it?

KATHERINE. Thursday.

JAMES. Hold it till Sunday? You'll get a better crowd. You'd prefer a big audience, would you no?

KATHERINE (*falters*). I...

JAMES. Course you would. Sunday it is, straight after mass. Outside the cathedral. Couldnae be better. Right. Settled.

Drink?

KATHERINE. I... What?

JAMES. You'll take a glass with me.

KATHERINE. I've not been sentenced.

JAMES. Och we can go back in for that. Let them wait. Let's us just have a blether first.

He's fixing drinks.

Or you think they might find you innocent of heresy? How're they going to do that? Unless you deny your heresy.

Are you going to do that?

KATHERINE. No.

JAMES. There you go then. Execution on Sunday.

What I've come to wonder is why we *burn* people for heresy. I'm not sure it's the most appropriate sentence. What're your thoughts?

KATHERINE. I…

JAMES. See, we burn folk for treason. We burn wives for murdering their husbands… deid witches… obviously, but *heretics*? Is it effective? I mean how does it look, to an audience.

How will it look, to your audience?

We hear the beginnings of noise outside, a distant mob gathering, it remains faint but surges under the dialogue.

I'm no advocating leniency across the board, you understand. Always have burnt people alive, always will burn people alive, terrifically effective deterrent to serious crime. My worry though, my worry is it'll become *particularly* associated with heresy, something about evoking the flames of hell maybe?

So then if people die *well*. Your brother put on a terrific show by all accounts – do we plant the idea that the flames are not… appropriate?

KATHERINE *has abruptly had enough.*

KATHERINE. Can you just stop with the 'burning alive' chat?! Can we?! I mean, there's been a lot, you know? I'm well aware. I've made my peace. These are my last hours. Great. Can everyone just *stop* with the 'burning to a crisp' conversation! I am *bored* at this point. Terrified, great, well done, boys, but I'm *bored* of terror.

So just…

Find a better conversation or shut the fuck up!

(*Afterthought.*) Your Majesty.

JAMES *is stunned.* SPENCE *is on. We're aware again of the sounds outside.*

SPENCE. Your Majesty…

JAMES (*to* SPENCE *but still completely on* KATHERINE). Yes, I know. In a minute.

KATHERINE. And you have met me by the way. And Patrick. You came trotting up to Kincavel on your fat little pony and turned our whole household upside down trying to get you a wee roasted sparrow. That was your fancy. We'd to pluck and roast a sparrow to give your royal mouth a wee tasty morsel and nothing else would do…

SPENCE. Majesty.

JAMES (*to* SPENCE). Shhh.

(*To* KATHERINE.) I've no recollection of eating sparrow…

KATHERINE. No, well, have you tried catching one? Then you were rampaging through the rooms, you smashed our best ashet because you didnae like its colour, you did your business behind my mother's chair…

JAMES. How old was I?

KATHERINE. How should I know. Ten? I was only five, I'd never seen anyone behave like that.

JAMES. What makes you think you can talk to me like that?

KATHERINE. I'm a dead woman! What're you going to do to me?

JAMES. If you're ready to die, why did you remind us that you're family to half the men in that room… and to me.

KATHERINE. To show them this isn't something crazy 'other' people are thinking. Folk just like them are seeing the truth. They need to see that, they need to…

(*Trying to gather her words.*) Patrick had his courage. I've none of that, I'll die badly, cannae be helped so –

JAMES. So…?

KATHERINE (*bursting out with it*). *I must be seen! I will be remembered!*

SPENCE. There's a crowd gathering outside. We've been advised to clear the court.

JAMES (*to* SPENCE). I'm sure the guards can hold the doors for the wee minute I need here.

(*To* KATHERINE.) Thing is, burning women are no great novelty.

They burnt the Lady Glamis for treason and witchcraft a few years back, you mebbe don't remember, I was just a bairn. That was my first burning, which'll be why *I* remember it, but who else does now? And she was a powerful woman, well known, rich… Are any women remembered? Men remember their mothers or their lovers but no one else records their names. Maybe if someone killed a queen it'd make a mark, but I think you're already invisible, darling, just a wee bonfire without a name.

SPENCE. It's the students outside, they…

JAMES. I know it's the students! *Of course it's the fucking students! Wheest*, will you!

(*To* KATHERINE.) So, as I said, the world's ending, that's clear. Some say Scotland started sliding into the abyss the day my father died. Which makes my accession to the throne one of the harbingers of the apocalypse. That's a nice idea to give a bairn as a christening gift, eh? It's possible this is all my fault, I mean he's deid, I'm *here*, cannae be his fault, eh? Must be mine. Everything's been my fault since I was seventeen months old and they whacked a crown on my heid but I don't *think* this one's on me. The whole of Europe's tearing itself to bits. The Pope is shitting it. You've no idea, you want to read the papal proclamations I'm getting. He cannae just tell a king what to do any more, he's got to *wheedle*. Now where's that gonny end? The earthly voice of God, *wheedling*. Nae bugger's really scared of ex-communication any more, are they?

Indicates the sounds of unrest outside.

I mean none of the folk that matter, the boys wi *education*. But they should be.

Aye, you hear them? Do you know what your brother did? He roused the students, the *students,* the young learned men o' money who were to be our priests and bishops and lawyers and men o' parliament. He's turned them into that rabble out there screaming for reform.

The Bishop of St Andrews was chased into his palace the other day. They caught two of his servants and set fire to their robes... I *think* they're still alive but they're no very pretty. A priest in Ratho was beaten senseless last night. He will die I think and that mob out there will likely hang someone today.

(*Indicating* SPENCE.) Hopefully him.

The Church is getting shaken to pieces. Of course it is. It's a mess. Half our bishops are still waiting for their balls to drop, the other half are rolling around in nests of whores or catamites... or both... Used to be this wasnae my problem, used to be I just tried to find good, loyal men to be our bishops, lived in fear of God, like any other good Christian, and said whatever the Pope wanted.

Now? The Pope's wheedling, the archbishops are quaking behind their locked doors and there's no one left to tell me what to do but the likes of *him*.

Indicating SPENCE *again.*

SPENCE. I have prayed for guidance, Majesty, and I will stand by you...

JAMES (*cutting him off*). Shut it! You had *one* job!

So it's all on me, eh? I have to stop the world ending.

Which means I have to take a guess at what God wants us to do.

(*Anticipating their disbelief.*) I know.

But that's the job! Good thing I like a gamble, eh?

We need order, we need peace, we need *you* to recant.

KATHERINE. You think that'll stop them?

JAMES. I think it'll *confuse* them. I think it'll slow them down.

And I don't believe you're ready to die.

KATHERINE. Of course I'm not! And I won't die well. But if I can have a wee bit of my brother's courage, that's all I need.

I know my duty, now.

JAMES. Well… it's nearly winter. Perhaps we do need a warming right enough.

And it'll certainly scare anyone keen to follow your defiant example.

(*Considers*.) Could go either way. More riots or retreat. Wee experiment. Dangerous… but that'll keep me sharp, eh?

SPENCE. Katherine, remember the faith you were born into, remember the shape of the God who loved you as a bairn, his true form. Please…

Suddenly JENNY *erupts*.

JENNY. I thought God was supposed to be mysterious!

You've nae idea what God is! What God wants! Any of you! How could you?

I cannae read but I know *crazy* when I see it. Just *stop it*!

JAMES. Do you know. I'd actually forgotten you were sitting there. You kind of blend in, eh? Who are you?

JENNY. Jane Spottiswood. Patrick's wife.

JAMES. Oh *you're* the wife!

JENNY. Aye. I'm the widow.

JAMES. Widow, widow, sorry.

(*Looking at her*.) A devout little heretic, is it time for your wee blasphemous squeaks then?

KATHERINE. Jenny has affirmed the Church's faith! Ask your Constable!

JENNY. No! I have not! I don't believe any of you!

SPENCE *despairs*.

SPENCE (*to himself*). Oh sweet Mary mother of God...

JAMES (*to* JENNY). Is that right?

JENNY. No! I don't! And that's fine! I understand I'm such a wee speck in creation, understanding will ay be beyond me, but how come you've all lost that sense?!

(*Turning on* KATHERINE.) And how does it go? 'We all really only get two choices, how we live and how we die.'

Really? *Really?* You think the beggarwoman out the door there chose to live in the gutter? You think she wants to die there? You think the wee boys sent to war *choose* to die wi spears in their thrapples? You think the poor lassies wi narrow hips *choose* to die when their bairns kill them? You think I chose this life? Fit to love no human creature but you that doesnae even love me enough to live?

But I tell you, Katherine Hamilton, I do still choose that, I choose to love you. Waste of me though that is. We all come to muck and worms but love is the only thing that lasts.

So here we go then. *Here* we go.

(*To* JAMES.) You want her you come through me.

KATHERINE. Jenny, don't!

JENNY. If they come for her... if you come for her... I'll stop you.

JAMES. Oh you'll *stop* me? Wi your wee fists and your wee kicking feet?

JENNY *is now holding on to* KATHERINE.

JENNY. Aye, I'm a joke, eh? I'm a wee joke! But I'll hold her.

JAMES. What do you think'll happen to you if you kick your king?

KATHERINE. Don't hurt her!

JENNY. I'll hold on to her, you'll not get me from her side...

JAMES. Oh I think I will, let's get the guards in...

KATHERINE (*under this*). No! She's just a bairn! She doesn't know what she's saying...!

JAMES (*over* KATHERINE). I reckon two men will prise you off, three tops, shall we try that?

JENNY. I'll no lose her again! Even if you burn me with her!

JAMES. *Great* idea! *That* would terrify them! Double bonfire! Spectacular! Let's do that!

KATHERINE (*cuts him off*). I recant!

I...

They both wait. She is struggling.

I will...

I acknowledge the authority of the true Church.

JAMES *thinks about it.*

JAMES. But I think I might just have heard a better offer...

See, if I burn her *too*, they'll understand I might burn *anyone*. I'll be a monster but *so* terrifying. Terror is good. It's effective.

KATHERINE *is desperate.*

KATHERINE. I'll kneel. I'll weep, I'll *beg*. I'll beg to be forgiven my heresy.

JAMES. Hmmm.

He considers.

Thing is... I do like you. I do. You're *loyal*. That counts for quite a lot.

He considers.

Will your recantation be convincing enough to slow this runaway cart?

And perhaps I am a monster. Perhaps that was always what God intended me to be? But mercy could feel sweet…

KATHERINE. I'll deny any truth you want.

KATHERINE *drops to her knees.* JAMES *decides.*

JAMES. Might work, might not, wee experiment. God will decide!

Good. Exciting.

(*To* SPENCE.) Do your job then.

After a moment, SPENCE *goes to* KATHERINE *and holds out crucifix and ring.*

SPENCE. Do you recant your heresy?

KATHERINE. I do.

SPENCE. Do you acknowledge the authority of the true Church and of her servants appointed by God?

KATHERINE I do.

(*She starts to cry.*) Oh God forgive me I do.

SPENCE. Do you reject the heresies of your brother and do you affirm that you know he burns in hell?

JAMES. Let's not push it, eh?

SPENCE *looks at* JAMES *and decides not to push it.*

SPENCE. Do you accept my authority to offer you God's absolution and the authority of the Mother Church's bishops, archbishops and of the Holy Father himself?

KATHERINE. I do.

KATHERINE *is talking to Patrick's memory though the words work for her recantation.*

Forgive me! Please, please, forgive me.

JAMES. She repents. Happy ending.

He comes closer to KATHERINE, *studying her.*

Do you think he will? Forgive you?

Do you think God will forgive any of us?

KATHERINE *remains kneeling, slowly getting herself back together.*

JENNY *comes closer to her. The noise outside is suddenly really loud. Hammering on the door and door bursting open.*

SPENCE. They've broken into the court.

JAMES. Aye.

I know the sounds of rage and panic when I hear them.

(*To* KATHERINE.) Those boys won't be happy with you, will they?

I think I'm best going out the back way…

He's moving off, they all follow him. He stops them.

(*To* KATHERINE.) Oh no no no no. *You're* no invited. You need to explain yoursel to your brother's loyal and godly followers, don't you? Just wait here. They'll find their way through here in a minute.

(*To* SPENCE.) See that she waits for them.

JAMES *leaves.*

The noise outside grows. SPENCE *has already decided what he must do, gathering his courage.*

SPENCE. Just wait a bit longer, then follow the King. I have to stand against this mob. This is the ecclesiastical court, they can't riot in here.

KATHERINE. You can't stop them!

SPENCE. I can. God is with me. I feel him. I can do this.

Now JENNY *is trying to leave, trying to get* KATHERINE *away.*

JENNY. Katherine! Come away!

KATHERINE (*to* SPENCE). You can't!

SPENCE. Someone has to stand up to them! God will protect me as I'm protecting his truth.

KATHERINE. They might kill you!

SPENCE. Well then I'll come to bliss.

JENNY. *Katherine!*

> JENNY *pulls* KATHERINE *away.*
>
> *We see* SPENCE *facing the door from the courtroom.*
>
> *We hear the mob, we know they're rushing at him.*
>
> *He holds his ground and raises his crucifix…*

SPENCE. Oh here we go then, here we go.

In the name of God! In the name of God!

Clifftop by the Sea

KATHERINE *and* JENNY *are on a path above the sea.*

They are hurrying from Edinburgh, escaping.

JENNY *has fallen behind.* KATHERINE *stops for her.*

KATHERINE. Come on!

JENNY (*breathless*). I cannae…

> KATHERINE *hurries back to her.* JENNY *tries to catch her breath.*

Where are we going?

KATHERINE (*points*). Down there, to the docks. I've enough money on me for the boat.

JENNY. Boat to where?

KATHERINE. Berwick-upon-Tweed.

JENNY. We're running away? Together?

KATHERINE. We have to.

> We have to leave everything we own and everyone we know and we cannae look back.

JENNY. Alright.

> Good.
>
> I'm ready for that.
>
> Are you?

KATHERINE. I…

> I'll have to be.

JENNY. I'm sorry, I'm so sorry.

KATHERINE. What?

JENNY. I made you recant, I made you lie.

KATHERINE. I didnae lie.

JENNY. What?

KATHERINE. I didn't lie.

> I didnae love Patrick's words enough to die for them.
>
> I love you too much to let you be hurt.

JENNY. See that's how I feel about you.

KATHERINE. Still?

JENNY. *Of course still!*

KATHERINE. But mebbe…

> *She hesitates.*

JENNY. What?

KATHERINE. Mebbe we're unnatural and we're damned.

JENNY. Mebbe.

But if we cannae love like this in paradise, why would we want to go?

KATHERINE. Do you think the students killed him?

JENNY. I hope not.

No.

But he's likely sair hurt. I cannae understand it. The world's breaking in bits.

I think there's mair to come.

KATHERINE. Aye.

JENNY. Will they chase after us?

KATHERINE. I don't know.

JENNY. I don't think there'll be a safe place in all of Scotland. For anyone.

KATHERINE. So we run. We've no choice.

JENNY. That was always my choice, to run, with you.

KATHERINE *is looking down at the harbour below.*

KATHERINE. That boat there, it will take cargo to Dunbar and on to Berwick, I know the captain. He won't betray us.

JENNY. But you don't want to go.

KATHERINE. I do. We have to. I want to.

JENNY (*seeing* KATHERINE*'s distress*). So what is it?

KATHERINE. I failed him.

JENNY. Patrick?

KATHERINE. Aye.

JENNY. No. He wanted you to live.

He asked me to save you.

I will always save you, if I can.

And I *don't* believe we're damned. Not if God made sunshine. Not if God meant us to love at all.

KATHERINE. I don't know who I am, Jenny. I don't know what'll become of the world. I don't know what'll become of me, now.

JENNY. Is that no how we're ay supposed to live?

It's a braw toon, Berwick. You'll love it. It's between everything. Between land and sea, soaring sky and craggy earth, you can choose your view in Berwick. Look up or down, inland or out to sea, see the weather changing every moment.

No certainties. Lots of choices.

And the border's close. You can stand with one foot in each country. If the English come to kill you, you can hop to Scotland, if the Scots are after you, you can hop back to England. Just a wee skip to keep you safe.

KATHERINE. Good.

JENNY. We'll be safe, Katherine. I'll keep you safe, and you me.

And if we cannae do that I'll still love you... Till we're deid, and after that who knows, so why worry?

And how are we unnatural?

Cats. Our brown tabby was crazy for the grey, rolling all over each other all day...

Two nanny goats we have yet, you cannae pen them apart...

House sparrows! Wee quine spuggies! I've seen them kissing beaks and preening each other and...

KATHERINE *has slumped*.

Sorry.

I'm just wittering on 'cause I'm happy. I'm happy you're no deid.

Can you be happy about that?

KATHERINE. Aye.

If God can forgive me…

JENNY. Doesn't God forgive us all?

KATHERINE. Maybe not… any more.

JENNY. Then do you need to listen to him?

KATHERINE. Mebbe I don't.

But then what do I live for?

JENNY. For my sake?

KATHERINE. For your sake?

JENNY. Just for a while.

Just if you feel you can.

As KATHERINE *still doesn't respond.*

No just for pity.

Just if you know the worth of me, Katherine Hamilton.

Because if you cannae look at the braw wee package of all I am and feel your soul melting in longing… I dinnae want you near me anyway, I…

KATHERINE *kisses her.*

KATHERINE. Shoosht.

Kisses her again.

Aye. I'll try that.

For your sake. For you, Jenny.

They hold each other, JENNY *hears something overhead. She looks up.*

What is it?

JENNY. Geese, flying south.

KATHERINE. Let's get after them.

She hugs JENNY *a moment more*.

Good news.

JENNY. What?

KATHERINE. We're alive, today.

End.

www.nickhernbooks.co.uk

facebook.com/nickhernbooks

twitter.com/nickhernbooks